MEGA MACHINE DRIVERS

This is my
tractor

Written by Chris Oxlade
Photography by Christine Lalla

W

FRANKLIN WATTS
LONDON • SYDNEY

This edition 2009

Franklin Watts
338 Euston Road
London NW1 3BH

Franklin Watts Australia
Hachette Children's Books
Level 17/207 Kent Street
Sydney NSW 2000

Editor: Jennifer Schofield
Designer: Jemima Lumley
Photography: Christine Lalla, unless otherwise acknowledged
Tractor driver: Charlie Murray

Acknowledgements:
John Deere: 7, 15, 17b, 18, 19, 20, 21, 23, 25, 26, 27b
The Publisher would like to thank Steve Mitchell, Charlie Murray
and all at John Deere for their help in producing this book.

A CIP catalogue record for this book
is available from the British Library.

ISBN: 978 0 7496 8918 6
Dewey Classification: 629.225'2

Printed in China

Franklin Watts is a division of Hachette Children's Books,
an Hachette Livre UK company.
www.hachettelivre.co.uk

Contents

My tractor and me

Hello! I am a tractor driver.
This is my tractor.

My tractor helps me
to do jobs on my farm.

> Tractor power

All the parts of my tractor are worked by the engine.

∧ *This is the engine.*
It is big and powerful.

The engine needs fuel to work.
The fuel is stored in the fuel tank.

The tank is made of very tough plastic.

Wheels and tyres

The giant wheels let me drive over muddy and bumpy fields.

My tractor's wheels are almost as tall as me!

▲ The tyres have a
chunky pattern so they
can grip in the mud.

Adding machines

I often put special machines onto my tractor for jobs on the farm.

< Farming machines go on the back of the tractor.

> This spinning rod from the engine makes the machines work.

Some machines are very heavy.
This weight at the front stops the
tractor tipping backwards.

Picking up

This is how I pick up a farm machine.

 *First I reverse up to the machine.*

Then I fix the machine to the tractor.

▼ Now I can lift up the machine to carry it along. This machine is called a disc harrow.

In my cab

I sit in the cab to drive my tractor. The cab keeps me warm and dry.

cab

> The cab has big windows so that I can see all around when I am driving.

∨ At night I turn on the bright spotlights on my cab.

Cab controls

The cab is full of controls for driving and working different machines.

I use the steering wheel to turn to the left or right.

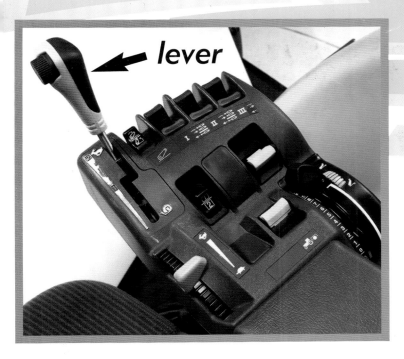

lever

<This lever lets me drive along at different speeds.

There are lots of switches here. Some work the tractor's lights. Some work farm machines.

Collecting hay

Today, I am collecting hay from my fields.

△ *This machine is called a baler. It rolls hay into bales.*

◁ *I carry the bales with a bale fork on the front of the tractor.*

▽ *Now I am towing away the bales on a trailer.*

Ploughing

We use a tractor to plough a field.

∧ *The tractor carries the plough to the field.*

< *This part is called a plough blade.*

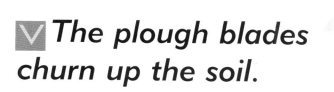 *The plough blades churn up the soil.*

More tractors

Here are some of the other machines I drive.

This giant tractor has tracks instead of wheels.

A combine harvester collects crops from my fields.

Be a tractor driver

It takes lots of practice
to become a tractor driver.

*You have to learn how to drive
the tractor safely along bumpy
farm tracks and on the roads.
You also have to practise towing
trailers.*

You have to learn about all the tractor's levers and switches.

You have to learn how to work farm machines and how to put them onto the tractor.

Tractor parts

spotlights

cab

window

engine
(inside)

6920 S

JOHN DEERE

weight

tyre

fuel tank

> Word bank

disc harrow – a machine that breaks up soil and makes it level

fuel – the liquid that burns inside an engine

hay – grass that has been cut and dried

plough – a machine that churns up soil in a field

reverse – go backwards

spotlight – a light that makes a beam like a powerful torch

tracks – the loops of metal or rubber links that some tractors have instead of wheels.

trailer – a vehicle that is pulled along by a tractor

Web fun

John Deere tractors have a great website, especially for children. Log on at: http://www.deere.com/en_GB/fun_zone/index.html

Index